SUMATRAN TIGERS AT RISK
SAVING THESE FIERCE BIG CATS

BY KATHRYN CLAY

CAPSTONE PRESS
a capstone imprint

Published by Capstone Press, an imprint of Capstone
1710 Roe Crest Drive, North Mankato, Minnesota 56003
capstonepub.com

Copyright © 2025 by Capstone. All rights reserved. No part of this publication may be reproduced in whole or in part, or stored in a retrieval system, or transmitted in any form or by any means, electronic, mechanical, photocopying, recording, or otherwise, without written permission of the publisher.

Library of Congress Cataloging-in-Publication Data is available on the Library of Congress website.

ISBN: 9798875222115 (hardcover)
ISBN: 9798875222061 (paperback)
ISBN: 9798875222078 (ebook PDF)

Summary: Sumatran tigers may be fierce, with sharp teeth and claws, but they are at risk of extinction. Readers will learn what is putting these big cats in danger, including hunting and a shrinking habitat, as well as what people are doing to help them.

Editorial Credits
Editor: Ashley Kuehl; Designer: Elijah Blue; Media Researcher: Rebekah Hubstenberger; Production Specialist: Tori Abraham

Image Credits
Alamy: Roy Cruse, 19; Getty Images: Aprison Photography, 7, CHAIDEER MAHYUDDIN/AFP, 23, George Pachantouris, 21 (Balkan lynx), Ger Bosma, 6, Ibrahim Suha Derbent, 21 (Amur tiger), iStock/MGPhotos, 5, iStock/ Muhammad Yasir, 28, iStock/slowmotiongli, 13 (top), 16, 17, iStock/Wirestock, 21 (African cheetah), Jeff J Mitchell, 18, Jefta Images/Future Publishing, 22, Lonely Planet, 21 (South China tiger), Mike Powles, 11, Ulet Ifansasti, 24, 25; Shutterstock: Dchauy, 21 (Asiatic lion), DeawSS, 4 (heart icon), Eric Isselee, 21 (leopard), imranhridoy, 4 (trees icon), JordanCrosby, 14, josefauer, 15 (buttons), Juanma66, 21 (serval), La Terase, 12, Mega Pixel, 15 (pencil sharpener), mxdsgn, throughout (tiger head icon), neelsky, 8, nexusby, 4 (temperature icon), Stefan Balaz, 4 (arrow icon), Viktor Tanasiichuk, 13 (map), Yadav Anil, cover; Superstock: Juniors Bildarchiv/juniors@wildlife Bildagentur GmbH, 9

Design Elements
Shutterstock: Pixels Park, Textures and backgrounds

Any additional websites and resources referenced in this book are not maintained, authorized, or sponsored by Capstone. All product and company names are trademarks™ or registered® trademarks of their respective holders.

Printed and bound in China.   006276

TABLE OF CONTENTS

CHAPTER 1
A DAY IN THE LIFE......................5

CHAPTER 2
GET TO KNOW SUMATRAN TIGERS.......10

CHAPTER 3
ENDANGERED.............................20

CHAPTER 4
HOW TO HELP............................26

GLOSSARY 30
READ MORE 31
INTERNET SITES 31
INDEX 32
ABOUT THE AUTHOR.......32

Words in **bold** are in the glossary.

WHAT MAKES AN ANIMAL ENDANGERED?

NUMBER OF ANIMALS:
VERY LOW OR SHRINKING FAST

HABITAT LOSS:
BIG DECREASE IN NATURAL HABITAT

RANGE REDUCTION:
SHRINKING AREA WHERE IT CAN LIVE

BREEDING DECLINE:
FEWER ANIMALS HAVING YOUNG

THREATS:
HIGH RISK OF POACHING, DISEASE, OR CLIMATE CHANGE

CHAPTER 1
A DAY IN THE LIFE

Evening settles over the dense forest in Indonesia. A tiger rises from its resting spot. The hungry cat is ready to hunt. It uses its sharp eyesight and hearing to search for prey. Once it spots prey, the tiger approaches. A quick pounce leads to a good meal. With a full belly, the tiger retreats to a hidden spot. The tiger rests as the sun rises.

A Sumatran tiger looks for prey.

A Sumatran tiger sharpens its claws on a tree.

Sumatran tigers are big cats. They live only on the island of Sumatra in Indonesia. Sumatran tigers are much smaller than other tiger **species**. They are known for their bright orange coats with narrow black stripes. The colors help them blend into their dark forest habitat.

Tigers prefer to live alone. They mark areas with their scent. That tells other animals to stay away. Tigers are night hunters. They move silently through the jungle.

TIGER TRIVIA

QUESTION: How do tigers mark their areas?

ANSWER: They drop urine or feces to leave a scent. They also leave scratch marks on trees.

A tiger peers down from a tree.

AT RISK

Tigers hunt and live alone. Their solo lifestyle makes them difficult to track. Scientists can only estimate their population size. But scientists agree that the species is severely threatened. Some researchers believe fewer than 400 Sumatran tigers remain in the wild. This fact puts them on the critically **endangered** list.

Some people kill Sumatran tigers for their fur and skin.

Poachers sell the bones and teeth of Sumatran tigers.

Poaching is the biggest threat. Sumatran tigers are targeted for their skins, bones, and other body parts. Despite **conservation** efforts, poachers continue to track and capture these tigers. Their actions put tigers at great risk.

CHAPTER 2
GET TO KNOW SUMATRAN TIGERS

Sumatran tigers are the smallest tiger species. Males weigh 220 to 310 pounds (100 to 140 kilograms). Females are lighter at 180 to 300 pounds (82 to 136 kg). These tigers are great hunters. Their size lets them move swiftly through thick forests.

TIGER TRIVIA

QUESTION: What tiger species is the largest?

ANSWER: Amur tigers are largest. They can grow to twice the size of Sumatran tigers.

The Sumatran tiger's whiskers and white fur sets it apart from other tigers.

Sumatran tigers look different in other ways too. At 6 to 8 inches (15 to 20 centimeters) long, their whiskers are longer than most tigers'. The whiskers help them feel around on dark forest floors. Males have long white fur around their necks. The color stands out against the black stripes, giving the tiger a fierce look.

Sumatran tigers live in thick forests, lowlands, and swamps. They are rarely active during the day. Instead, they choose shady spots to rest. At night, they are ready to hunt. The darkness helps them stay hidden and sneak up on prey.

A tiger's **territory** depends on how much prey is available. They are known to travel long distances if food is scarce. Unlike most large cats, tigers are strong swimmers. They swim across rivers or swamps to find food or mates.

Most tigers can hold their breath underwater for up to a minute.

TIGER TRIVIA

QUESTION: How far will a tiger travel to find food?

ANSWER: Up to 18 miles (29 kilometers).

Sumatran tigers are **carnivores**. They eat mostly deer and wild boars. They also eat monkeys, fish, birds, and small mammals. These skilled hunters wait for the perfect moment to strike. Sometimes they silently stalk their prey for hours before pouncing. Tigers can eat up to 65 pounds (30 kg) in a meal. They won't eat again for several days. They hide leftovers for another day.

A Sumatran tiger eating its prey

BLENDING IN

Learn how blending in helps tigers sneak up on their prey.

MATERIALS

- Several small objects in different colors, including green and brown
- Timer or stopwatch
- Notebook and pencil

STEPS

1. Go outside and choose an area with plants, grass, or dirt.

2. Scatter the small objects around the area.

3. Set a timer for five minutes. Try to find as many objects as possible. Write down how long it took you to find each object. Note which ones were easier to find.

4. Write down what you learned. Which objects blended into the environment? How easy were those to find?

LIFE CYCLE

Sumatran tigers live alone. They only come together to mate. Cubs are born after about three and a half months. Each litter has two to four cubs. They are born blind. It takes six to eight weeks for them to see well. Until then, they depend on their mother.

Female tigers raise cubs alone, providing food and protection. Within a few months, the cubs start following their mother on hunts. She helps them learn survival skills. After two years, the young tigers leave their mother's territory. Males often travel farther away. Females tend to stay closer.

Mother tigers carry their cubs by the scruff of their neck.

Sumatran tiger cubs learn to hunt from their mothers.

TIGER TRIVIA

QUESTION: What is the lifespan for Sumatran tigers?

ANSWER: Sumatran tigers live 10 to 15 years in the wild and up to 20 years in captivity.

WEAPONS AND DEFENSES

Sumatran tigers have powerful body parts that make them excellent hunters. Their sharp claws help them grab prey. At 4 inches (10 cm), each claw is about the length of a crayon. Their teeth are slightly shorter. Tigers can easily tear through meat and bones. These defenses keep tigers safe from other animals. But they are no match for determined poachers.

Tigers have the biggest canine teeth of all cats. Canine teeth are the long, pointy ones.

Tiger cubs often fight for play. But adult tiger fights are usually real.

Tigers don't usually use their claws and teeth on other tigers. But if they have a reason to fight, they may attack. This may happen when a male goes into another male's territory. Male tigers might also fight when trying to impress a mate. A mother tiger might attack if another tiger gets too close to her cubs.

CHAPTER 3
ENDANGERED

A species is considered endangered when not many are left. Only about 400 Sumatran tigers are left in the wild. They are at high risk of becoming **extinct**. They could disappear forever. Humans have created many challenges to tiger survival. Without taking steps to protect them, we risk losing tigers for good.

TIGER TRIVIA

QUESTION: How are tigers and snowflakes similar?

ANSWER: Every snowflake has a unique shape. Each tiger has a different pattern of stripes.

BIG CAT CONSERVATION

Many big cat species are endangered. The list below includes some of the most vulnerable cats.

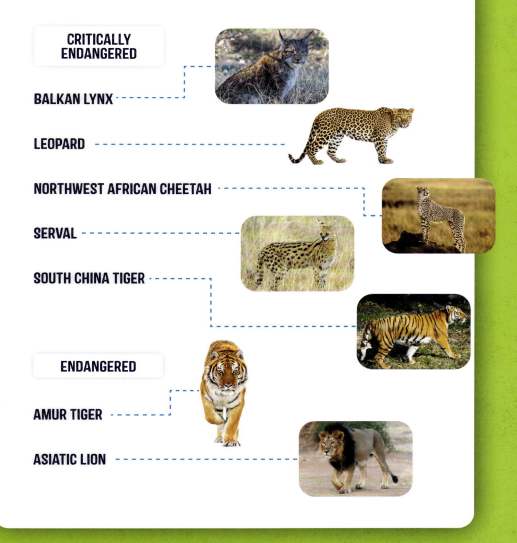

CRITICALLY ENDANGERED

BALKAN LYNX

LEOPARD

NORTHWEST AFRICAN CHEETAH

SERVAL

SOUTH CHINA TIGER

ENDANGERED

AMUR TIGER

ASIATIC LION

HUMAN-MADE RISKS

Humans create the greatest risk to all tigers. Poachers hunt tigers to sell their skin, bones, and teeth. It is illegal to sell tiger parts. But laws are not always followed. It is easy for people to poach tigers when habitats don't have enough guards. TRAFFIC is a group that tracks poaching data. They've recorded nearly 3,500 tigers killed by poachers since 2000. And that is just the tigers that were discovered. Many others were likely **smuggled** successfully.

A police officer in Indonesia holds Sumatran tiger teeth. The poachers who killed this tiger were arrested in 2015.

A forest ranger in Indonesia holds up a tiger trap he found in the rainforest.

ENVIRONMENTAL RISKS

One big problem is deforestation. This is when people cut down trees to make space for farms and buildings. When tigers' homes are destroyed, they have nowhere to live. As more people move into tiger habitats, conflicts between tigers and humans are more likely.

Deforestation strips land bare.

The Kerumutan rainforest in Sumatra is protected. But that doesn't stop loggers from setting up camp and cutting down trees illegally.

Climate change is another threat. Weather changes can harm the forests where tigers live. Rivers may dry up or get polluted. That can hurt the animals that tigers eat. All these risks make it harder for Sumatran tigers to survive.

— CHAPTER 4 —
HOW TO HELP

Kids can play an important role in tiger conservation. One way to help is to learn more about tigers. They can share knowledge with friends and family. Understanding why tigers are important can inspire others to care about them too.

Another way to help is to support organizations that protect tigers. Donating money or holding fundraisers can help. People can organize a walkathon or fun run. They can collect donations for every lap or mile. Friends can join in. The money raised can go to tiger conservation groups.

GROUPS WORKING TO HELP SUMATRAN TIGERS

CONSERVATION INTERNATIONAL
This part of Wildlife Conservation International supports the conservation of endangered animals in Indonesia and Southeast Asia.

WORLD WILDLIFE FUND
This group works to protect and replant forests in Sumatra and conducts research on wild tigers.

PANTHERA
This group researches wild cats and educates local communities about them. They design and build technology to catch poachers.

GLOBAL TIGER INITIATIVE
This group studies tigers and threats to them. They train people who live near tigers to protect them.

INTERNATIONAL FUND FOR ANIMAL WELFARE (IFAW)
This group rescues animals and rebuilds habitats.

Palm oil is made from palm fruits.

Kids can take action in their own communities too. They can join local clean-up events or plant trees. Keeping nature healthy helps all animals, including tigers. Avoiding certain products can help stop deforestation in Indonesia. One of the biggest problems comes from palm oil companies. They cut down trees to make room for plantations. Choosing products without palm oil can help protect forests and animals. Products that may contain palm oil include snack foods, ice cream, peanut butter, and dog food.

Every little bit counts. By working together, people can make a difference for these amazing creatures.

MATCH THE TIGER

STEP 1: Species Cards: Make six cards. Write a tiger species on each.

STEP 2: Unique Features Cards: Make six more cards. Write a unique feature of one tiger species on each.

STEP 3: Mix up the cards. Then try to match each species card with its unique feature card.

Bengal tiger	Bright orange coat with dark black stripes
Amur tiger	Largest tiger species
Sumatran tiger	Smallest tiger species; has a furry face
Malayan tiger	Narrow stripe pattern
Indochinese tiger	Dark fur with lots of stripes
South China tiger	Oldest tiger subspecies

GLOSSARY

carnivore (KAHR-nuh-vor)—an animal that eats other animals

climate change (KLYE-mit chaynj)—changes to weather patterns and a global increase in temperature caused by human activities

conservation (khan-sur-VAY-shun)—wise use and protection of natural resources

endangered (en-DANE-jurd)—at risk of dying out

extinct (ik-STINGKT)—no longer living; an extinct animal has died out.

poaching (POHCH-ing)—illegal hunting or fishing

smuggle (SMUHG-uhl)—to take something into or out of a country illegally

species (SPEE-sheez)—a group of plants or animals that share common characteristics

territory (TER-i-tor-ee)—an area of land controlled by an animal or group of animals

READ MORE

Eason, Sarah. *Saving the Tiger*. Bridgnorth, UK: Cheriton Children's Books, 2023.

Geister-Jones, Sophie. *Tigers*. Mendota Heights, MN: Apex, 2022.

Wolf, Debra Kim. *A Family for Zoya: The True Story of an Endangered Cub*. Washington, DC: Platypus Media LLC, 2025.

INTERNET SITES

10 Terrific Tiger Facts!
natgeokids.com/uk/discover/animals/general-animals/10-tiger-facts/

Sumatran Tiger
ran.org/wildlife-factsheet/wildlife-fact-sheet-sumatran-tiger

Sumatran Tiger
zooatlanta.org/animal/sumatran-tiger/

INDEX

claws, 6, 18, 19
climate change, 4, 25
conservation, 9, 20, 21, 25, 26, 27, 28
cubs, 4, 16, 17, 19

deforestation, 24, 25, 28

fundraising, 26
fur, 8, 11, 29

habitats, 4, 6, 12, 22, 24, 25, 27
hunting, 5, 7, 8, 10, 12, 14, 16, 17, 18

mating, 4, 12, 16, 19
palm oil, 28
poaching, 4, 9, 18, 22, 27

scents, 7
size, 6, 10

teeth, 9, 18, 19, 22

whiskers, 11

ABOUT THE AUTHOR

Kathryn Clay has written more than 100 nonfiction books for kids. Her books cover a wide range of topics, including everything from sign language to space travel. When she's not writing, Kathryn works at a college, helping students develop their critical thinking and study skills. She holds master's degrees in literature and creative writing from Minnesota State University, Mankato.

Kathryn lives in southern Minnesota with her family and an energetic goldendoodle. Together, they make sustainable, eco-friendly choices whenever possible.